NO WAY!

CRAZY BUILDINGS

Michael J. Rosen

and Ben Kassoy

Illustrations by Doug Jones

Millbrook Press • Minneapolis

WAYWARD WONDERS
THE CROOKED HOUSE AND THE DANCING HOUSE

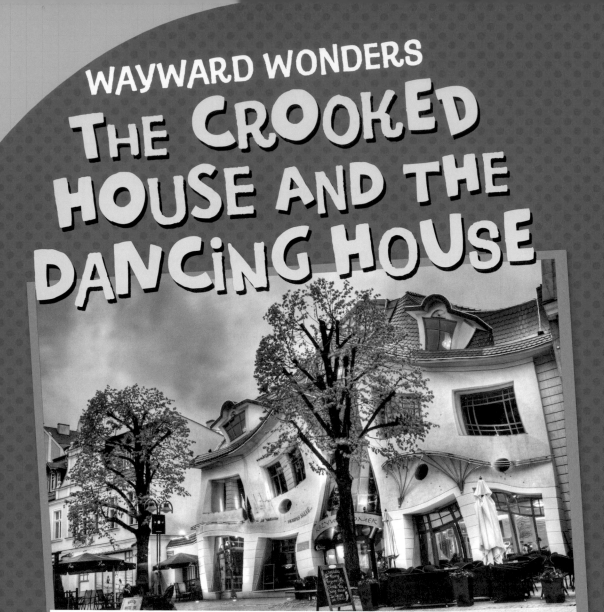

Once upon a time, in a faraway land, a man built a magical house.

Well, the time was 2003. And the land was Poland, which may not even be far from where you live. Okay, and the place wasn't *exactly* magical . . . or even really a house. Even so, the Krzywy Domek [KRIHZ-eye DOH-mehk], or Crooked House, looks as if it's part of a fairy tale. The architect was inspired by the folktales he loved as a boy.

The Crooked House is misshapen and odd. The structure appears to be melting. Is the building tired of standing up straight? If the Crooked House were one of the seven dwarfs, it would definitely be Sleepy!

So far, no Cinderella has made the Crooked House her castle. Instead, you'll find shops and restaurants. Grab a bite and browse around. (No promise that you'll find that perfect glass slipper.)

The Crooked House is the main tourist attraction of the city of Sopot. Onlookers wonder whether it's real. Some even hesitate to step inside. They're afraid they'll be pulled into a make-believe land. Yikes!

The Dancing House in Prague, Czech Republic, is another wayward wonder. The building resembles a pair of performers. One building leans over with flexibility and grace. The other building stands strong. It appears to support its partner in a gravity-defying duet.

The Dancing House was built in 1966. It was inspired by the famous dancers Fred Astaire and Ginger Rogers. "Fred and Ginger" became the perfect nickname for towers that seem to be tangoing.

One side of Prague's Dancing House dips like an actual dancer.

CAVE-MUNITIES
ROCK HOUSES AND VILLAGES

Pop quiz: what are troglodytes [TRAH-gloh-dytes]?

Nope, not aliens from an old movie. Nope, not cousins of the cockroach.

They may sound monstrous, but troglodytes are simply people who live in caves. So maybe they're more like bats. But cave dwelling isn't batty. People have done it for thousands of years!

From the 500s B.C. to the A.D. 400s, southern Jordan was home to the Nabataean [nah-BAH-tee-ihn] people. Their capital was the amazing sandstone city of Petra. *Petra* is Greek for "rock"—and does this city ever rock! Houses, temples, theaters, and tombs were built into the region's reddish cliffs. Architecture throughout Petra is standing after twenty-five hundred years.

The peoples of Petra *(left)* and Cappadocia *(right)* lived in custom-carved rock dwellings.

Rocks kept houses warm in the winter and cool in the scorching Middle Eastern summer. The Nabataeans also created a complex system of pathways called aqueducts to bring water to the sandstone city.

Here's another quiz question: what's a fairy chimney?

No, not how the tooth fairy slips into your house. It's a dwelling place left by a volcanic explosion!

Millions of years ago, volcanoes erupted in Cappadocia [CA-peh-doh-shuh], Turkey. Lava from the volcanoes hardened into rock. Then, many years of wind and rain formed a skyline of pointed peaks from the rocks. These fairy chimneys soar into the sky.

Underneath Cappadocia's majestic towers lie underground cave cities. Human beings carved out these dwellings. In the eleventh century, they protected thousands of local troglodytes from attackers. The big, bad wolf would have to *really* huff and puff to blow *this* house down!

NAUTICAL NEIGHBORHOODS
HOUSEBOATS

You wake up. You look out the window. And . . . your house has moved! No, there wasn't a tornado. You live on a houseboat! Overnight, the tides nudged your home a few yards away.

This happens to all houseboats. Some are called non-cruising boats. They're permanently tied or anchored to a dock. Others are blue-water boats. Outfitted with an engine or sail, they're a fully mobile home away from home!

There are many floating communities around the world. In these seaworthy suburbs, families live in quaint homes that line quiet sidewalks—er, *sidedocks.*

A houseboat has everything most grounded houses possess. Only the names are different. Your bed? It's a "berth." Your bathroom? It's the "head." And instead of a pool in your backyard, your backyard *is* a pool—big enough for waterskiing!

Even if you have a TV, you'll spend less time battling your sibs for the remote and more time fighting for the helm. That's the steering wheel of the houseboat. Of course, you'll need permission from your parents. (You'll have to call them Captain and First Mate.)

Sometimes, a house *becomes* a boat. And not on purpose. A hurricane can uproot a home and sweep it out to sea. So the architects at Morphosis are creating a house that floats— but only when necessary. In case of high floodwaters, this home is designed to glide up 12-foot (3.6-meter) guideposts and float safely. The house also breaks away from electric lines and plumbing, so residents can rise above whatever nature throws down.

WOODSY WONDERLAND
THE WORLD'S LARGEST TREE HOUSE

In the Bible, Noah hears a heavenly message: A flood's coming. Build a giant ark (boat) and bring on board two of every animal.

Architect and Christian minister Horace Burgess says he heard a similar command. In 1993 he began building his modern-day ark in Crossville, Tennessee. It's wood. It's enormous. But the only animals aboard are humans. Oh, and it doesn't float anywhere. Behold the Minister's Tree House!

As Burgess explains, he was told, "If you build me a tree house, I'll see you never run out of material." Burgess turned his vision into a reality. His creation is the largest tree house on Earth.

This tree house in Crossville, Tennessee, rises 97 feet (29 m) into the sky.

Burgess used recycled materials. He took lumber from torn-down buildings. He accepted donations. The project still cost Burgess nearly $12,000. Sound like a big number? Not compared to a quarter *million*. That's how many nails he used in the ten years it took to build his ten-story tree mansion.

With an 80-foot (24 m) white oak for a foundation, the house stands 97 feet (29 m) high. It branches out nearly 10,000 square feet (929 sq. m). The Minister's Tree House is practically its own forest.

Inside, there's a space for visitors to pray, with rows of pews and a choir loft. There's also a top-floor living space, a basketball court, and a half-ton chime. The house is free and open to the public. Most weekend afternoons, you'll find kids playing hide-and-seek, waiting for a turn on the swing, or just gawking at this woodsy wonderland.

11

HOME IS WHERE THE DOG IS
DOG BARK PARK INN

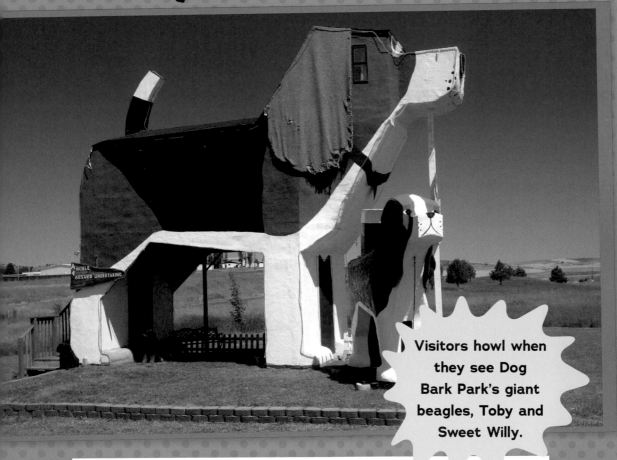

A NOBLE ABSURD UNDERTAKING

Visitors howl when they see Dog Bark Park's giant beagles, Toby and Sweet Willy.

Normally, being "in the doghouse" means being in trouble. No doggone fun. Not so at Cottonwood, Idaho's Dog Bark Park Inn. It's home to the world's largest beagles!

A 12-foot-tall (3.6 m) beagle named Toby stands outside this attraction. Yes, Toby is one mighty hound sculpture. But he's less than half the size of his 30-foot-tall (9 m) beagle pal Sweet Willy, who doubles as a bed and breakfast!

Artists Dennis Sullivan and Frances Conklin began work on Dog Bark Park in 1997. The duo used money they had made selling chainsaw carvings of dogs to build the pair of giant pooches.

Four people at a time can comfortably fit inside Sweet Willy. Guests walk up a flight of stairs and enter the living room through his belly. His head houses the top floor. His snout is a cozy nook. Sweet Willy is also decked out in doggy decorations. Visitors can check out the owners' famous wooden chainsaw carvings. Book yourself a night in this comfy kennel, and you may never want to sleep in a plain old house again.

And remember: Toby and Willy are only two examples of quirky roadside buildings across the United States that resemble other objects. For a home shaped like a spaceship, blast off to Chattanooga, Tennessee. To see a house that looks like a pickle barrel, visit Grand Marais, Michigan.

SHELL SHOCK
NAUTILUS HOUSE AND CONCH SHELL HOUSE

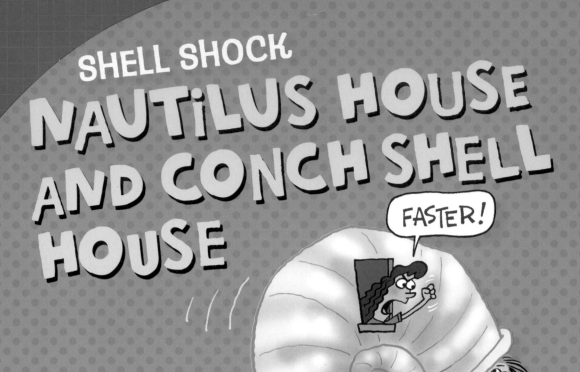

FASTER!

For a snail, life moves—you've got it—at a snail's pace. After all, you have to lug your whole home around. Things get downright sluggish. But life can be swell in a house-sized shell!

Take the Nautilus House of Mexico City, Mexico. It looks like a real snail shell. And like a snail's shell, this building is one sturdy shelter. Its 2-inch-thick (5-centimeter) concrete walls make it nearly earthquake-proof.

Mexico's Conch Shell House *(right)* and Nautilus House *(opposite page)* are spiral-shaped twists on home design.

The house is composed of many natural features. Within the Nautilus, a stone sidewalk lines a "carpet" of leaves and grass and snakes its way from room to room. The bathroom's blue tiles and overhead window make this beachy abode appear to be under the water. Most spectacular of all, stained-glass windows dot the house's walls. On the inside, the shining sun creates a new rainbow every day!

To see another shell, travel east to Mexico's Isla Mujeres [ees-LAH moo-HAIR-ehs]. You'll find the artist Octavio Ocampo's famous Conch Shell House.

This home is shaped like one giant, spiky shell. It's shaped from many little ones too. More than four thousand shells from local beaches line the house, from the bedroom to the kitchen and everywhere in between. Even the bathroom sink is made of a conch. Its faucets? Pure coral.

The Conch Shell House—which is for rent!—provides a sweeping view of the sea and a pool. Talk about a relaxing vacation. At this place, you can return from a day at the beach . . . to the beach!

What has no corners, a thousand windows, and a forest for a roof? The Waldspirale (vahld-SPEE-rah-leh)! This apartment complex in Darmstadt, Germany, is not your average dwelling. It looks more like someone's wacky art project than a tower of rental units.

Friedensreich Hundertwasser designed the building in the 1990s. This Austrian artist was anything but traditional. His other famous apartment complex, Hundertwasser House in Vienna, Austria, is a collage of colors. Tenants get to paint the outside of their apartment in any manner they'd like.

The Waldspirale is a multicolored, U-shaped curiosity. What are those shining onion-shaped domes doing there? That's got to be a mistake! Those belong on Russian churches!

If you keep looking, the twelve-story building offers even more oddities. Each window is unique. All one thousand of them. They aren't placed in a pattern either. In the architect's words, the windows are "dancing out of line." Some windows have trees poking out of them! And the building's slanted roof is planted with a garden of grasses, shrubs, and flowers! (*Waldspirale* is German for "forest spiral.") With all these natural elements, the Waldspirale continues to grow and change long after its construction ended.

Doorknobs and window handles throughout the building's 105 apartments are as odd as the windows. Many are decorated in Hundertwasser's colorful style. With every corner of the building rounded, the Waldspirale certainly echoes the architect's philosophy of going "against the straight line."

The walls of Waldspirale feature windows that were placed willy-nilly.

HOME ON THE STRANGE
HAINES SHOE HOUSE

There was an old woman who lived in a shoe... That's just a nursery rhyme, right?

Turns out that a footwear fortress actually exists in Hellam, Pennsylvania. Colonel Mahlon M. Haines built the Haines Shoe House in 1948. The Shoe Wizard, as he was called, handed an architect an old work boot and said, "Build me a house like this." Somehow, the architect took the request in stride!

The Shoe House was built upon a wood frame. That frame was covered with wire and coated with thick stucco. The finished building stands 25 feet (7.6 m) tall and 48 feet (14.6 m) long. The colonel used this spectacle to market his shoe-store chain.

The place is a showcase for shoes, and a *boot*load of fun. Three bedrooms, two baths, a kitchen, and a living room squeeze into the shoe's five levels. There's a shoe for a mailbox, a shoe-shaped doghouse, and a stained-glass portrait of Haines—holding shoes—on the front door.

Early on, Haines invited elderly couples or honeymooners to stay for a weekend. He provided them with a maid, a cook, and a driver. They received new outfits and free footwear. Haines would even *foot* the bill. These days, anyone can take a tour through the shoe house. Come have homemade ice cream in the shoe's sole!

Businessman and footwear fan Mahlon M. Haines left his footprint on the world with the Haines Shoe House.

HAINES
THE
SHOE WIZARD

INSIDE A TREE ORNAMENT
FREE SPIRIT SPHERES

The Free Spirit Spheres in Vancouver Island, Canada, are like little worlds within the island's thick rain forest. Inventor Tom Chudleigh created the spheres. He believes that "the magical environment of the forest . . . [brings] up thoughts of elves and fairies." You might think of monsters too. The spheres resemble giant eyes peering at passersby.

Chudleigh handcrafted each of his three spheres from wood. "I wanted to enable people to . . . [live in] the forest without taking it down first," he says.

He based their design on biomimicry. That means they imitate a shape that occurs in nature. "The sphere is nature's packaging," he says. He points to the nutshell and eggshell as examples. Where did the name come from? Well, Chudleigh says he made the spheres for "the untamed spirit that exists in us all."

For guests, the spheres provide a cozy shelter . . . 10 or 15 feet (3 or 4.6 m) in the air. Guests have their pick of the spheres Eryn, Eve, or Melody. Each ball is tied to trees by a web of ropes. Inside each sphere is a tree-houselike setup. Well, more like a tree hotel room.

Guests climb a spiral staircase to reach their sphere. Rounded windows give a glimpse of the forest. Skylights welcome sunbeams. The wind blows and the sphere sways.

The Free Spirit Spheres aren't short on luxuries. Visitors will find a microwave, a refrigerator, a sound system . . . oh, everything except a bathroom. Good thing you're surrounded by woods!

ROCK STEADY
IDEAL PALACE

At age fifty-five, Ferdinand Cheval was known to his neighbors in Hauterives, France, as a postal worker. Or as a dreamer. After his death at eighty-eight, he was called a genius. Over the course of three decades, Cheval built his legend from the ground up.

During his daily 20-mile (32-kilometer) mail route, Cheval daydreamed of building a "fairy-like palace beyond imagination." One day in 1879, he stumbled upon his inspiration. Cheval tripped over a rock with such an interesting shape that he took it home. Soon he began collecting rocks every day. The hobby added an extra 6 miles (9 km) to his route. That was the start of Le Palais Idéal (LUH pal-AY ee-DAY-ahl), the Ideal Palace.

Visitors to the Ideal Palace can say thanks to Ferdinand Cheval.

Locals doubted and mocked him. What did he think he was doing? Cheval had no idea. "I was not a builder," he admitted. "The chisel was unknown to me. Not to mention architecture, a field in which I remained totally ignorant."

Cheval was a self-taught artist. He studied books for inspiration. He found simple building materials. Historians say he toiled somewhere between sixty-five thousand and ninety-three thousand hours over the course of some ten thousand days. Thirty-three years after he began, Cheval completed a masterpiece of hard work and technique.

Cheval's palace is a wondrous mixture of structures. Some parts resemble ancient Asian temples. Others look like European castles or designs from Hindu mythology.

"Should there exist a more determined man than myself," Cheval once said, "then let him set to work."

No takers? Didn't think so.

DiG THESE DUG-OUTS
UNDERGROUND DWELLINGS

In *The Hobbit,* author J. R. R. Tolkien describes the dwellings of hobbits as comfortable, homey holes in the ground. These fictional lairs have inspired dozens of real-life underground homes. The buildings are popping up from the rolling hills of New Zealand to the beachfronts of Florida. Make that popping *down.*

Many underground homes are built into the side of a hill. Covered in grass, they nestle into the landscape. If you lived there, you wouldn't just mow the lawn. You'd mow the roof!

So where did Tolkien get his inspiration? The Vikings. The author based his hobbit homes on traditional Norse architecture. Hundreds of years ago, people in Norway, Sweden, and Denmark lived in underground houses with sod-grass roofs. Picture a hill with windows! Newfoundland,

A Kansas couple poses at the entrance tunnel to a house and former missile silo.

Canada, offers a look at these dwellings. Newfoundland's modern L'Anse aux Meadows house was rebuilt from the traces of a station for Norse explorers.

Some underground homes were meant to be anything *but* homey. During the Cold War (1945–1991), the U.S. government prepared for nuclear war with the Soviet Union. The military built huge underground silos to store nuclear weapons. When the threat ended, the missiles moved out—and families moved in!

One hideaway near Topeka, Kansas, once housed a giant nuclear bomb. These days, it houses . . . a house! What happened to the space that stored the 40-foot-long (12 m) missile? It's the garage. How about the former control area? It's the living room. And the kitchen? It's still big enough to feed an army!

STONE, SWEET STONE

HOUSE OF STONE AND JOSHUA TREE BOULDER HOUSE

The House of Stone stands between four giant boulders in Portugal's Fafe Mountains. Sure, you can spot the stones... but what about the tiny crooked windows and rusty roof?

This stony home was built in 1974 as a family's summer retreat. For a time, few people had actually seen the house. The place looked so unbelievable in photos that many wondered whether it was real. Much of the two-story home's interior still remains a mystery to most fans. Some say it even houses a pool!

Portugal's House of Stone is a mysterious mountain dwelling.

You'd think thick stone walls would be enough to fend off tourists and burglars. Guess not. The owner installed a steel door and bulletproof windows for extra privacy and security.

A two-bedroom home in California has an even bolder design. Or should we say *boulder!*

Joshua State Park is famous for its magnificent boulder formations. Nearby, you can see the amazing, human-made Joshua Tree Boulder House. That is, if you can find the place.

From the front, the 1,700-square-foot (158 sq. m) home is camouflaged by the surrounding desert. Visitors have a tough time telling the house's human-made boulders from the area landscape.

Circle around back, and the house's open-air porch leads to a blend of natural wonder and modern luxury. Outside, there's an open-air fire pit. Inside, there's a heating and cooling system built into the floors. Living in the Joshua Tree Boulder House, you're definitely not stranded in the desert.

OFF THE DEEP END
MARiNA BAY SANDS HOTEL

What's the best part about staying at a hotel? The pool! So what's the best part about staying at the world's coolest hotel? The world's coolest pool!

Come take the plunge at Marina Bay Sands Hotel in Singapore, where guests feel as if they're swimming on cloud nine! Perched atop the hotel's three fifty-five-story towers is the world-famous SkyPark. And on top of that? A breathtaking pool that's as long as three Olympic-sized pools. You'd probably deserve a medal for swimming a single lap!

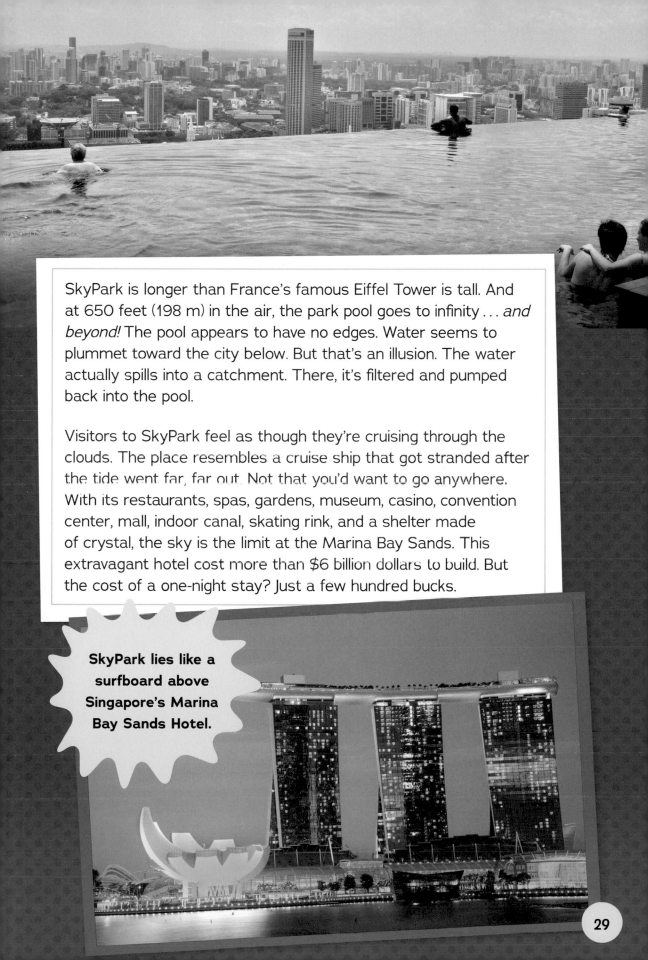

SkyPark is longer than France's famous Eiffel Tower is tall. And at 650 feet (198 m) in the air, the park pool goes to infinity . . . *and beyond!* The pool appears to have no edges. Water seems to plummet toward the city below. But that's an illusion. The water actually spills into a catchment. There, it's filtered and pumped back into the pool.

Visitors to SkyPark feel as though they're cruising through the clouds. The place resembles a cruise ship that got stranded after the tide went far, far out. Not that you'd want to go anywhere. With its restaurants, spas, gardens, museum, casino, convention center, mall, indoor canal, skating rink, and a shelter made of crystal, the sky is the limit at the Marina Bay Sands. This extravagant hotel cost more than $6 billion dollars to build. But the cost of a one-night stay? Just a few hundred bucks.

SkyPark lies like a surfboard above Singapore's Marina Bay Sands Hotel.

GLOSSARY

abode: a home or a place to stay

aqueduct: a passageway that carries large volumes of water from one place to another

architect: a person who plans and oversees the construction of buildings or other structures

bed and breakfast: a small hotel in which guests are offered a room and a morning meal

boulder: a very large rock, often round in shape

camouflage: a disguise that uses colors or patterns that blend in with an environment

collage: a visual mix or blend

conch: a sea animal that lives within a spiral-shaped shell, or the shell itself

fairy chimney: a tall, slender tower of rock formed by many years of wind and rain

inspire: to guide a person's actions or to excite a person into action

Norse: relating to the people or culture of medieval Scandinavia, a region that includes Norway, Sweden, and Denmark

nuclear: using the power of atomic energy

resemble: to look like

rotate: to turn in a circle or to follow in a certain order

silo: a tower-shaped structure

sphere: a round, three-dimensional object such as a globe or a ball

stucco: a type of plaster applied to walls or ceilings

tango: a ballroom dance from Latin America

tenant: a person who rents a house or a place of business

Viking: any of the Scandinavian peoples whose ships raided the European coast from the eighth century to the eleventh century

SOURCE NOTES

11   Horace Burgess, quoted in "Crossville Tree House to God Still a Work in Progress," July 14, 2012, http://www.knoxnews.com/news/2012/jul/14/crossville-tree-house-to-god-still-a-work-in (March 11, 2013).

16   Friedensreich Hundertwasser, "Hundertwasser on Hundertwasser," 1975, http://www.hundertwasser.at/english/hundertwasser/hwueberhw.php (March 11, 2013).

18   Mahlon M. Haines, quoted in "Heines Shoe House," RoadsideAmerica.com, n.d., http://www.roadsideamerica.com/story/2202 (March 11, 2013).

20   Tom Chudleigh, "All about Spheres," Free Spirit Spheres, n.d., http://freespiritspheres.com/all_about_spheres.htm (March 11, 2013).

22   Ferdinand Cheval, quoted in "Palais Idéal, Hauterives, France," PBS, 2013, http://www.pbs.org/independentlens/offthemap/html/travelogue_artist_4.htm?true (March 11, 2013)

23   Ferdinand Cheval, "The Ideal Palace of Cheval Postman," France.com, October 24, 2008, http://www.france.com/general/the_ideal_palace_of_cheval_postman (March 11, 2013).

FURTHER READING

BOOKS

Arbogast, Joan Marie. *Buildings in Disguise: Architecture That Looks Like Animals, Food, and Other Things.* Honesdale, PA: Boyds Mill Press, 2010.
Take a tour of structures that were built to resemble other things. From Lucy the Margate Elephant to the Longaberger Company's seven-story basket-shaped building, twenty-four buildings are profiled with cool photos and postcards.

Kerns, Ann. *Seven Wonders of Architecture.* Minneapolis: Twenty-First Century Books, 2010.
This book in the Seven Wonders series features fun facts about extraordinary structures such as the Taj Mahal, the Eiffel Tower, and Chicago's Willis Tower. For more on crazy buildings, check out *Seven Wonders of Engineering* by Ron Miller.

Laroche, Giles. *What's Inside?* Boston: Houghton Mifflin, 2009.
This book begins with a teasing question and goes on to reveal the mysteries of fourteen remarkable landmarks. Learn more about the Tomb of Tutankhamun, the Parthenon, the Guggenheim Museum, the Sydney Opera House, and the Georgia Aquarium. *What's Inside?* includes detailed drawings and paintings.

WEBSITES

BUILDING BIG

http://unusual-architecture.com
This blog collects images and information about the world's strangest churches, houses, libraries, concert halls, and other architectural marvels. Check out photos, descriptions, interesting facts, and related links.

UNUSUAL ARCHITECTURE

http://www.pbs.org/wgbh /buildingbig
This site ties into the five-part PBS series *Building Big.* Try *Building Big's* interactive games and "lab projects," and find out more about bridges, domes, skyscrapers, dams, and tunnels.

INDEX